Dorset's

and

Fortifications

by
Robert Hesketh

Inspiring Places Publishing
2 Down Lodge Close
Alderholt
Fordingbridge
Hants
SP6 3JA

ISBN: 978-0-9928073-9-9
© Robet Hesketh 2017
All rights reserved
Contains Ordnance Survey data © Crown copyright and database right (2011)

Inspiring places
www.inspiringplaces.co.uk

Contents

3   Iron Age Hillforts

8   Roman and Romano-British Fortifications

10   Anglo-Saxon Defences

11   The Norman Period, 1066 - 1154

21   The Later Medieval Period, 1154 - 1485

28   Tudor Fortifications, 1485 - 1603

32   The Civil Wars, 1642 - 1651

32   Victorian Fortifications

39   Second World War Fortifications

40   Castles as Luxury Homes

42,43   Map of Locations

44   Bibliography

Front cover: Lulworth Castle (by kind permission of Lulworth Estate).
Rear cover: Corfe Castle.
All photos by the author, except pg 39 by Robert Westwood.

Iron Age Hillforts

Among English counties, Dorset has a particularly rich heritage of Iron Age hillforts. Characteristically, these are ditch and rampart structures. Following the natural contours of the land, they occupy high strategic vantage points, with panoramic views and include many of Dorset's highest hills such as Pilsdon Pen (277m/914ft), Lambert's Castle (258m/851ft) and Eggardon Hill (252m/832ft). Sites with steep slopes were favoured, making attack difficult and costly. Surrounding trees and vegetation were cut back to make surprise assault almost impossible.

Spoil from the ditches provided material for the ramparts, which were often fortified with timber palisades. These have fallen victim to time, whilst wind and rain have partly flattened the ramparts and filled in the ditches.

All the same, Dorset's Iron Age hillforts remain immensely impressive and a tribute to the Durotriges, the Iron Age people who occupied Dorset and gave the county its name. Probably, growing tensions, related to increased population pressures and a more hierarchical, competitive society, led people in the Iron Age (circa 800BC to 43AD) to invest a huge amount of time and labour in hillforts.

Hillforts, like later Anglo-Saxon burghs (page 10) and medieval walled towns, sheltered resident populations within their defences. They also provided refuge for people living and working in the surrounding area if conflict broke out.

Badbury Rings.

Christchurch Harbour from Hengistbury Head.

"In the reign of Claudius….Vespasian was transferred to Britain, where he fought thirty battles with the enemy, subjugated two powerful nations, and more than twenty towns", wrote Suetonius in *The Lives of the Caesars*, 121AD. For "towns" we may read "hillforts".

Evidence of attack on Dorset hillforts has been found at Hod Hill and Spetisbury and more Roman ballista bolts (iron spearheads) were discovered at Waddon Hill and Pilsdon Pen. However, Dorset's hillforts were built centuries before the Roman invasion to meet threats from other Britons.

This is most evident in West Dorset, where a string of hillforts, including Pilsdon Pen, Coney's Castle, Lambert's Castle, and Eggardon Hill face the Devon border, formerly the territory of the Iron Age Dumnonni who occupied modern Devon and Cornwall. East Devon has a corresponding series of hillforts including Membury, Musbury, Blackbury, Hembury, Sidbury and Woodbury.

Iron Age hillforts occupy strategic sites throughout Dorset, including coastal forts at Abbotsbury, Flowers Barrow and Bindon Hill. East Dorset has a chain of Iron Age forts, including Hambledon Hill, Hod Hill, Spetisbury Rings, Buzbury Rings and Badbury Rings, with the Double Dykes on Hengistbury Head opposite Christchurch Harbour at the southern end.

Hengistbury Head's fortifications were designed to protect one of Iron Age Britain's key ports, exporting slaves, hunting dogs and precious metals, and importing luxury items such as wine, olives and glass. Rich archaeological finds strongly suggest Hengistbury Head was also an important mint and metal working centre. Its earthwork defences consisted of an inner bank 3m (10ft) high, with a ditch 3.5m (11.5ft) deep. An outer ditch 6m (20ft) wide and 2m (6.5ft) deep has been covered by sand and silt. *Hengistbury Head, Southbourne, SZ163912, BH6 4EN. Open during daylight. Some steep slopes and uneven ground.*

Maiden Castle is the largest and most complex Iron Age hillfort in Britain. Home to several hundred people during the Iron Age, its vast multiple ramparts enclose an area the size of 50 football pitches.

Occupation began around 4,000BC during the Neolithic (New Stone) Age. The hilltop was cleared of trees and an oval enclosure with two ditches constructed, possibly as a symbolic space for communal activities. This eventually fell out of use, but a huge 550m long mound, a "bank barrow", was built.

In the early Iron Age the site became a hillfort. Initially, it had only a single rampart at the eastern end of the hill and a small, self-sufficient community. Over the following 400 years, Maiden Castle grew to be the most important settlement in southern Dorset, with many roundhouses and greatly developed defences.

It was reconstructed on a much larger scale around 350BC with a single large rampart and two gateways. Around 250BC the camp was greatly extended again to its present 46 acres (19ha) to accommodate a much larger population. Maiden Castle was greatly re-fortified between 150 and 70BC when the early single rampart was heightened and two additional circuits built with stone revetments and cores, further strengthened by outworks.

Hambledon Hill Iron Age hillfort.

Designed to confuse attackers and expose them to volleys of missiles, these entrances – like the gatehouses of great medieval castles such as Corfe Castle (page 18) – no doubt served also as a deterrent and a display of power.

How effective was Maiden Castle when confronted with the best armed, trained and disciplined army in the Ancient World? Following the Roman invasion of Britain in 43AD, the 2nd Augustan Legion under Vespasian campaigned through southern England. The "war" cemetery at Maiden Castle excavated by archaeologist Sir Mortimer Wheeler in the 1930s has been taken as evidence of violent assault by the Roman soldiers.

Wheeler envisaged the Romans making a rushed assault in tortoise formation, their shields covering their heads, as they braved a hail of sling stones from the hoard of 22,000 found at the east entrance. Most of these were pebbles, but some baked clay balls. Examples can be seen at the Dorset County Museum in Dorchester. Wheeler concluded the Romans defeated and massacred

The mighty ramparts of Maiden Castle.

the defenders: the usual Roman practice with defeated people they regarded as barbarians.

The late Iron Age cemetery at Maiden Castle contains more than 52 burials. Some of the male skeletons suffered horrific injuries. Two are displayed in the County Museum, one with a Roman ballista bolt imbedded in his spine. However, not all the bodies show marks of violent trauma and the presence of grave goods including rings, brooches, pottery and joints of meat does not suggest they were buried hastily after a massacre. The battle scarred warriors may have been injured resisting the Romans, but it is possible that some at least were wounded in earlier, local conflicts.

Maiden Castle (English Heritage), Open during daylight. Some steep slopes and uneven ground. SY665885, DT2 9EY, 2 miles south of Dorchester, off A354. Dorset County Museum, High West Street, Dorchester DT1 1XA, 01305 262735. Monday-Saturday all year. www.dorsetcountymuseum.org

Roman and Romano-British fortifications

Vespasian crushed the Durotriges through superior tactics, weapons and discipline, but most of all by leading a united force. Whilst the Roman historian, Tacitus admired the hardihood and barbaric courage of the British tribes, he saw their lack of organization – both military and political – as a fatal weakness. "Nothing has helped us more in war with their strongest nations than their inability to cooperate. It is but seldom that two or three states unite to repel a common danger."

The Romans went on to establish a garrison at Durnovaria, the site of modern Dorchester. It is not clear whether there are remains of a fortress beneath Durnovaria similar to one built by the Second Legion in Exeter.

> **Roman Dorchester**
> Durnovaria was certainly well fortified, protected by a substantial earthen bank and multiple ditch system, enclosing some 70-80 acres (29-33ha). Later, a stone wall was built to front the bank. A short section opposite the main gate to the gardens in Albert Road is extant, and the wall line follows the garden boundaries. By the time of the Roman withdrawal from Britain, the walls reached 3m (10ft) high.
>
> The remains of the Roman town house in Colliton Park include an underfloor heating system and a beautiful mosaic. Both wall and town house are described in a leaflet offered by the *Tourist Information Centre, 11 Antelope Walk, DT1 1BE, 01305 267992.*
>
> **Bokerley Dyke** is a ditch and bank defence, 3½ miles (5.75km) long. Winding sinuously across the countryside, the Dyke forms part of the present Hampshire/Dorset border. It is thought to have originated in the Bronze Age or early Iron Age, but was remodelled in the later Iron Age and Roman periods, presumably to meet changing defensive or political needs. The Roman road from Sarum (Salisbury) to Badbury Rings which cuts through it was blocked in the fourth century AD, a time when Britain was under attack from Picts, Scots and Saxons. Later, the road was reopened. *Bokerley Dyke. Parking area at ST035202, Martin Down, A354. Access by public bridleway.*
>
> **Hod Hill** Early Roman forts have been found at Lake Gates, Bradford Abbas, Shapwick, Wimborne and Waddon Hill, where a Roman sword, scabbard and coins were discovered. Eleven ballista bolts were found at Hod Hill, where a camp was built within the existing Iron Age hillfort,

probably for auxiliary cavalry troops. This re-use of a good defensive site clearly demonstrated Roman dominance. The Roman camp occupies 200 square metres in the north-west corner of Hod Hill, its well defined rectangular lines suggesting clear purpose and military discipline for its 720 legionaries and auxiliaries.
Hod Hill, between Stourpaine (DT11 8TA) and Child Okeford, ST856106. National Trust. Parking. Access by steep footpath. Open during daylight.

Hod Hill.

Bokerley Dyke (mid-ground and top of hill).

The Romans abandoned Hod Hill fort about 50AD and Waddon ten years later. This suggests these and other Roman forts were temporary expedients as resistance was crushed. Roads were a more enduring Roman legacy. Everywhere the Romans went they built roads, both for military and later civilian purposes. Straight and direct as Latin prose, they included the main route from Sarum (Salisbury) to Dorchester and west to Exeter, as well as roads from Dorchester to Radipole, and Badbury Rings to the Roman port at Hamworthy in Poole Harbour.

Roman Town House, Dorchester.

Mosaic in Roman Town House.

Anglo-Saxon Defences

In 787 three Norse ships landed on Portland, according to *The Anglo-Saxon Chronicle*. The royal reeve came down from Dorchester to ask their business and they killed him on the spot. This proved to be the start of over 200 years of Viking attacks on England.

Alfred, King of Wessex from 871-899, was chiefly called "Great" for his successful resistance to Viking conquest. His establishment and organisation of thirty burghs (defended towns) throughout Wessex was crucial. Wareham and Christchurch were certainly burghs. Bridport and Shaftesbury were very probably burghs also.

A well-developed Saxon port, Wareham was an attractive target for the Vikings, who attacked and occupied it in 876. No doubt, this trauma greatly encouraged local people to support Alfred's ambitious plans to defend the town with massive earthen ramparts faced with timber.

> **Wareham's Wall Walk** provides the best example of Saxon town defences in England. The earthen ramparts still surround the heart of Wareham on three sides, whilst the River Frome blocks the south side and the river Piddle provides additional defence to the north. These defences were put to the test during the Civil War. Despite improvements to the town walls in 1642, Royalists took the town in 1643. However, Parliamentary troops retook Wareham in 1644, forcing their way through the West Gate in the walls. In 1940, the outer scarps of the defences were made steeper as a protection against tank attack, providing a remarkably recent example of fortification reuse.
>
> *Wareham's ramparts may be viewed in passing from the A351 or (much better) explored on a signed walk from Streche Road car park, Wareham BH20 4QF.*

Wareham's Wall.

Evidence of the fear and hatred felt towards the Viking attackers can be found at the County Museum, where one exhibit shows the remains of Vikings beheaded about 900. These skeletons were found with approximately fifty other Viking skeletons. All were butchered. The number executed is unparalleled among mass graves of this period.

In the late tenth century the Vikings stepped up their attacks and Wareham's defences were strengthened with a stone wall set on a mortared base in the existing earthen rampart. The stone wall was dismantled after the Norman Conquest and some of the stone was probably used to build the then new but now vanished Wareham Castle (page 14). Thus defence shifted from town walls to castle, clearly demonstrating the new Norman rulers valued their own power over the safety of their conquered subjects in Wareham.

The Norman Period, 1066-1154

After the Battle of Hastings in 1066, King William divided the land, titles and power taken from the defeated English and distributed them among his chief followers through the hierarchical feudal system, thus hoping to win their loyalty and support. He further secured the Conquest with a dense network of hastily erected castles, which were almost unknown in England, though familiar as bases of power and oppression in Normandy. Had England been defended with castles before 1066, the result of the invasion might have been quite different.

Be that as it may, the invaders needed castles as both bastions and administrative centres to dominate the local community. They were heavily outnumbered – an estimated 10,000 soldiers facing the hostile native population of between one and two million. Ideally, castles were spaced the distance a cavalry patrol could comfortably cover in a day - around eleven miles.

Erecting as many as fast as possible was an urgent task. England was racked by revolts every year from 1067 to 1070. The Western Rebellion of 1068-69 was not the least of these. English from the western counties loyal to King Harold's mother, Gytha, defended the walled city of Exeter and succeeded in negotiating favourable surrender terms with William – no mean achievement.

Castles were the local and very visible expression of Norman power, based on William's strong, centralised monarchy. Typically, they began as motte and bailey structures with wooden fortifications, often rebuilt later in stone. Unfortunately, Dorset has lost all trace of several Norman castles, including Wimborne, Stourton Caundle and Bridport. Some other Dorset castles have disappeared under later structures, including Lulworth Castle (page 40), Dorchester Prison and Shaftesbury Castle.

Among Dorset's surviving castles, it is often the mottes, the raised mounds on which the castles' last bastions or keeps were built, that are best preserved. Unsurprisingly, strong defensive positions on hilltops with steep slopes were often chosen.

Powerstock Castle occupies a strong defensive position on a hilltop with steep slopes. Its motte and bailey are further defended with ditches and ramparts. (On private land, but viewable from the footpath between Kings Lane and Castle Mill Farm.) *Powerstock Castle, SY521959, DT6 3TF.*

Cranborne Castle is another good example of a Norman castle, with a high motte and ramparts on a commanding hilltop position. Little is known of its history, though it was the property of Henry I's son, Robert. Half a mile north in Cranborne village is embattled Cranborne Manor, dating from 1207, but remodelled and extended into a country house in the seventeenth century. The manor's gardens are open to the public on Wednesday afternoons in summer. *Cranborne Castle, SU059127. Access by permissive path. Cranborne Manor, BH21 5PP, 01725 517248.*

East Chelborough Mottes A medieval motte and bailey occupies the top of Castle Hill at East Chelborough. Curiously, there is a separate motte nearby, just east of Stake Farm. Evidence is lacking to show the relationship between the two mottes or to be sure either was a castle proper rather than a ringwork, but it is possible the Stake Farm motte was replaced by the Castle Hill defence. (Both mottes are on private land, but Castle Hill can be viewed from the road, Stake Farm motte from the footpath opposite Manor Farm.) *East Chelborough, ST551054, DT2 0PZ.*

Christchurch Castle As well as asserting their authority throughout the land, England's new Norman masters protected the coast from attack by building castles at Christchurch, Wareham and on Portland. Christchurch (originally Twynham) was an Anglo-Saxon burgh refortified by the Normans. Its castle motte and ruined keep survive, despite being slighted on Parliament's orders in 1652, though the lodgings, kitchen, stables and chapel that occupied the outer bailey (defended area) are gone. However, the Norman House, with the lord's private apartments and great hall, are extant (see page 23). *Christchurch Castle, BH23 1AS, SZ160927. English Heritage. Open during daylight.*

Powerstock Castle.

Castle Hill, Chelborough.

Cranborne Castle.

Christchurch Castle.

Henry I's only legitimate son died in 1120. The king nominated his daughter, Matilda (otherwise called Maude), his heir, but she and her second husband, Geoffrey of Anjou, proved unacceptable to many of the king's leading subjects. When Henry died in 1135 his nephew, Stephen, seized the crown, opening England to civil war.

Stephen's reign, often called The Anarchy, was marred by almost continual warfare between Stephen and his cousin Matilda. Dorset was not immune from the violence. Baldwin de Redvers, Earl of Devon, held Corfe Castle for Empress Matilda, despite two sieges by King Stephen in 1138 and 1139 (see page 18).

Wareham's Norman castle was held by Matilda's half-brother, Robert of Gloucester, and withstood attack in 1138. However, it fell to a second attack when Robert was abroad in 1142, but he soon recovered it. In the same year, Robert took Lulworth Castle. He also took Rufus Castle from Stephen and ceded it to Matilda.

The struggle between King and Empress ebbed and flowed for the remainder of Stephen's reign. In 1153, the ageing Stephen, disheartened by the death of his wife and eldest son, accepted Matilda's son Henry as his heir in return for life possession of the throne. A generation of war had weakened royal power, whilst strengthening the barons. Thus the barons' castles became personal power bases and a real or potential threat to the Crown – a dangerous situation which Henry II (1154-89) addressed with his characteristic energy.

Rufus Castle (Bow and Arrow Castle) stands on a rocky pinnacle guarding Church Ope Cove on Portland. The original Norman castle was rebuilt in 1258. In its turn, this thirteenth century castle provided the foundations for the solid stone keep or blockhouse we see today. This was built in the mid fifteenth century by Richard, Duke of York. (The castle is on private ground, but readily viewed from the Coast Path and the beach.) *Rufus Castle, SY697712, DT5 1JA.*

Rufus Castle.

The gatehouse of Old Sherborne Castle.

Sherborne Castle England's Norman masters dominated the Church, which was immensely powerful and wealthy in pre-Reformation England. One of Dorset's most impressive Norman castles was built at Sherborne for a prince of the Church. Roger de Caen was Bishop of Salisbury 1103-1139 and, until 1122, Abbot of Sherborne. He also had great secular power as Henry I's Chancellor and deputised for the king. After Henry's death in 1135, Stephen seized Sherborne Castle. However, he surrendered it in 1143 after the Battle of Wilton to Robert of Gloucester to secure the release of William Martel, his loyal supporter.

Sherborne Castle was a great prize. Bishop Roger had built a palatial mansion for himself, as befitted his high religious and political status. As well as the Great Tower, he built the Great Hall, a double chapel and a range of domestic buildings. Visitors entered through the massive and imposing South West Gatehouse via a bridge across a dry moat. For defence, the middle section of the bridge could be removed. (In the thirteenth century, this was replaced with a drawbridge.)

Sherborne's domestic buildings were further protected by a wall 2m (6½ ft) thick and 7m (23ft) high, plus a ditch 20m (66ft) wide and a lake on three sides. Five towers provided flanking fire.

The Church had to wait until 1354 to recover Sherborne Castle. Bishop Wyville accepted single combat should determine the castle's ownership. However, the trial was postponed when the Bishop's champion, Richard Snawell, was discovered trying to gain unfair advantage with "rolls of prayers and charms" beneath his coat of mail. Snawell's opponent failed to show up for a second trial by single combat. Thus the Bishop won by default, though he had to pay 3,000 marks compensation to reclaim the castle too.

Sherborne Castle remained a bishop's residence until 1591 when Queen Elizabeth I obtained a 99 year lease. Within a year she transferred the lease to one of her chief favourites, Sir Walter Raleigh. Although Raleigh angered Elizabeth by seducing and secretly marrying Bess Throckmorton, one of her Ladies-in-Waiting, he regained the Queen's favour and enjoyed full possession of the castle from 1599.

Raleigh's aim was to make Sherborne Castle a suitably grand residence in the modern, Elizabethan style. He was probably responsible for demolishing the south range and altering the south-west gatehouse by adding windows. Dissatisfied with the results, Raleigh had a hunting lodge built, using stone from Old Sherborne Castle. This grew and developed

New Sherborne Castle.

into the splendid New Sherborne Castle, which was sold by James I to the Digby family in 1617 during Raleigh's imprisonment.

The damage Raleigh had inflicted on the Old Castle's defences was no doubt bitterly regretted by the Digbys, who held it for Charles I during the Civil War. Sherborne Old Castle was surrendered to a superior Parliamentarian force in 1642. Re-garrisoned for the King, it resisted General Fairfax's siege for sixteen days in 1645, but the Parliamentarians captured it after destroying one tower with artillery and breaching the east wall, forcing the Royalists to retreat to the central buildings. The Royalist soldiers were spared, but their goods seized and sold in Sherborne market. Like Corfe Castle (page 18), Sherborne Old Castle was slighted – deliberately damaged to render it indefensible. Wind, rain and further robbing of the castle's masonry have left the still impressive ruin seen today. Sherborne New Castle, however, remains a handsome Tudor mansion with beautiful gardens and archaeological finds from the old castle. *Sherborne Old Castle, English Heritage. ST648168, DT9 3SA, 01935 812730.*
Sherborne New Castle, ST651165, DT9 5NR, 01935 812072. Seasonal opening. www.sherbornecastle.com

Corfe Castle occupies a high, rocky hill with steep sides. It guards a gap in the chalk ridge, the obvious gateway to the Isle of Purbeck. One of England's most important royal castles, Corfe was built in several phases, and extended, modernised and strengthened using durable local limestone. Corfe probably began as a pre-Saxon fortified site. The later Saxon Hall is possibly the place where King Edward was murdered in 978, reputedly on the orders of his step-mother, Elfrida, thus clearing the path for her own son, Ethelred, to become king.

The Normans knew a superb defensive site when they saw one and built a thick stone wall to encircle the castle's Inner Ward from the beginning: a clear demonstration of its importance as most early Norman castles were built entirely of wood. However, the Norman builders did use wood for the palisades guarding the West Bailey and Outer Bailey, though they rebuilt the Saxon Hall in stone.

Henry I replaced the hall with the Great Keep in 1105. One of the earliest stone keeps built by the Norman kings in England, it stood a massive 21m (69ft) tall on top of the 55m (180ft) high hill and was strengthened with thick, high walls, towers and battlements.

One of the largest buildings that had ever been built in south-west England, Corfe stood as a daunting and impressive symbol of Norman power. Baldwin de Redvers described Corfe as "the most secure of English castles" and established himself there in defiance of King Stephen (1135-54). Stephen lost no time in excavating a ring and bailey fortification at Corfe Rings just south-west of the main castle. The earthen banks were topped with timber palisades and it is possible he may have attacked the castle with siege engines.

Corfe Rings are a rare example of a ring and bailey castle, a bank with a ditch outside and a platform or walkway inside. Perched on a hill 300m west of Corfe Castle, they command an excellent view of the castle, Corfe village and the roads leading into it. Despite these advantages, Corfe Castle proved too strong for Stephen and he gave up on both his attempted sieges in 1138 and 1139 to fight battles elsewhere. Over 500 years later during the Civil War, the Rings were temporarily re-used and some records refer to them as "Cromwell's Battery". *SY955820. Follow signed footpath SW of castle.*

Medieval kings were peripatetic, constantly moving around their kingdoms with their armed retinues to stamp their personal authority on each locality. Visits to Royal castles were a vital part of exercising that authority. King John (1199-1216) visited Corfe and used it as a prison and place of execution for his enemies. During his turbulent reign, castles were the single largest item of Royal expenditure and Corfe was high on the list. Not one to stint himself, John had a new Royal residence built at Corfe, the luxurious Gloriette.

His successor, Henry III (1216-1272), spent further large sums improving Corfe Castle. In the next reign, Edward I (1272-1307) added the outer gatehouse and further defences. By 1285, the castle was defended by stone walled enclosures and all its main defensive features were in place. Anyone entering or attempting to enter the castle had to pass by three gatehouses, defended with massive oak doors, portcullises, murder holes and galleries for archers.

It was equally difficult to leave Corfe without permission and the castle served as both a treasury and a high security prison. Unwilling guests included Henry I's brother, Robert Curthose and, in 1326, Edward II. As its military role declined from the fourteenth century onwards, Corfe was developed more as a residence and window glass (a great luxury) was installed in 1377.

Like Sherborne Old Castle (page 16), Corfe Castle was sold by Elizabeth I to a favourite, Sir Christopher Hatton, who used it as a country house. However, the English Civil War put Corfe Castle's defences to the test again. Lady Mary Bankes, wife of Sir John Bankes the Lord Chief Justice, held Corfe Castle for Charles I in her husband's absence and withstood two long Parliamentary sieges in 1643 and 1645.

Corfe Castle.

Corfe Castle.

In the first siege, 500-600 Parliamentarians were pitted against 80 defenders. The Parliamentarians reused Corfe Castle Rings as a base for their guns. After six weeks, the castle was relieved by Royalist troops. Whilst the attackers had lost 100 men, the defenders only lost two.

By 1645, Corfe was one of the last Royalist strongholds in the South. The castle was only taken after seven weeks when one of its Royalist defenders, Colonel Pitman, treacherously admitted enemy troopers. He had ostensibly left the castle to bring in reinforcements, but returned with Parliamentary soldiers disguised as Royalists. The next day, the Royalists found themselves under attack from within and without. A truce was agreed and Lady Bankes (now a widow) was allowed to leave with her garrison and keep the seals and key of the castle in recognition of her bravery.

Parliament feared Royalist strongholds might be refortified in a second civil war and ordered many to be "slighted". In 1646, a team of sappers led by Captain Hughes of Lulworth used explosives to render the castle useless for defence. It took them several months to ruin the work of six centuries.

In the following years, much of Corfe Castle's stone and fittings were robbed, often for buildings in the village. Nonetheless, it remains an extraordinarily powerful monument to England's medieval castle builders and the violent turmoil of the Civil War. *Corfe Castle, National Trust, BH20 5EZ, 01929 481294. Open all year. Slopes and steps.*

The Later Medieval Period, 1154 - 1485

King Henry II (1154-89), the first Angevin King of England, strove to end the anarchy of Stephen's reign and reassert royal authority. He destroyed some of the barons' castles and built some specifically royal castles such as Orford in Suffolk. He insisted castles could only be built or fortified by his permission with a licence to crenellate. In Dorset, Richard de Clare, Duke of Gloucester, obtained a licence to crenellate Rufus Castle in 1258. Holditch Court near Thorncombe was granted a similar licence in 1397, as evidenced by the surviving ivy covered tower.

Controlling castle building was wise. England was dominated by the power struggle between the barons and the monarchy, which erupted in the Barons' Wars of 1215-17 and 1263-67, despite the Magna Carta ("Great Charter") in 1215. One of the most celebrated documents in English history, Magna Carta was designed to prohibit arbitrary royal actions and assert the rights of subjects – above all the rebellious barons, who cajoled King John (1199-1216) into signing it.

Like King John, his son, Henry III (1216-72), spent heavily on building and improving royal castles, including Corfe. Much of his reign was occupied fighting for the real sovereignty of England with the barons who, led by Simon de Montfort, defeated him at the Battle of Lewes in 1264. Happily for Henry, his enemies quarrelled amongst themselves, paving the way for eventual restoration of order and a greater measure of royal authority.

Sometimes inspired by examples of more sophisticated Continental and Near Eastern castles seen by Crusaders, the later medieval period was a time when English castle architecture developed greatly. England's expanding population and trade helped fuel these developments, at least until the Great Famine (1315-17) and the even more terrible Black Death (1348 -1349), which may have killed a third of the English people.

The introduction of gatehouses, for instance at Corfe Castle and Sherborne Castle, was a notable development in military architecture, fortifying the vulnerable castle entrance and at the same time making it far more impressive and intimidating. Gatehouses were further protected by a portcullis, a sturdy spiked iron grille which was raised with a winch and served as another door to trap attackers – or it might be dropped on their heads. The slots for a portcullis can be seen at Sherborne Castle and the South-West Gatehouse of Corfe Castle. This Corfe gatehouse also displays the square holes for the draw-bars of the massive oak doors; the guardrooms of the men on duty and the charmingly named "murder holes" in the roof of the passage through which rocks, stakes and hot liquids could be dropped

Old Sherborne Castle.

on attackers. Stone blocks protrude from the upper walls. These supported galleries, allowing defenders to cover the base of the gatehouse with arrows and missiles.

Castles developed as high status residences and impressive statements of aristocratic wealth and power - or royal power and wealth in castles such as Corfe owned by the Crown. They were also administrative centres. Dorset's castles provide many examples of non-military additions.

King John's Gloriette at Corfe had no military purpose; it was in the castle's heart and amply defended. Its remnants show craftsmanship in this luxurious royal residence was comparable to that at Wells Cathedral. "Gloriette" means "highly decorated chamber" and King John would have had the rooms bright with tapestries and wall paintings. No doubt, the castle was bedecked with flags and pennants and a banquet prepared in the Great Hall when John arrived with his huge retinue to hunt deer and boar on Purbeck.

When the Norman House by Christchurch Castle was constructed about 1160, its chimney was an exceptional luxury. Before the sixteenth century, very few houses had complete upper floors and fires were usually on open hearths, the smoke simply rising upwards to escape through roof louvres, making the entire building smoky and odorous.

Another innovation was the garderobe, a small chamber for hanging clothes (as the name implies) or storing valuables. A garderobe might include, as it does at Christchurch, an indoor latrine, a chute between the inner and outer walls. Conveniently sited in the solar (private chamber), the Christchurch garderobe chute debouches into the mill stream.

The heart of the later medieval castle was the Great Hall. Again, the Christchurch Norman House, where the great hall's fireplace and decorated window survive, is a fine example. King John was a guest and likely dined here, reassured by the castle on the western side and the defensive curtain wall on the exposed eastern side. Moreover, all the doors and windows on the exposed side had draw-bars.

The lord's private chamber at Christchurch marked another improvement in material comfort. It also marked a new and growing social division, lamented by poet William Langland in "Piers Plowman". Langland favoured the old traditions of communal living and eating in hall for the lord and his entire household as celebrated in many Anglo-Saxon poems.

An Englishman's home is his castle and castles such as Corfe and Sherborne were luxurious. A little lower down the social hierarchy, houses such as Athelhampton and Wolfeton, as well as Sturminster Newton, Chideock and Woodsford Castles, appear to have been homes first and castles second and are sometimes described as "fortified manors". However, drawing a clear distinction between "castles" and "fortified manors" is difficult, especially as the terms are used loosely. It is really a matter of degree, depending upon whether defensive or domestic features predominate. The ravages of time, plus later alterations and demolitions often complicate the issue, leaving a lot of room for surmise and imagination when visiting these sites.

The Norman House, Christchurch.

Chideock Castle The first licence to crenellate the manor house at Chideock was granted in the late thirteenth century. Following the French raid on Weymouth in 1380, Sir John de Chideocke obtained a further licence to crenellate. During the Civil War, Chideock Castle was taken for Parliament in 1643, but re-taken by the Royalists the next year. In 1645 Parliamentarians from Lyme stormed the stronghold, capturing one hundred prisoners and thirty horses, plus powder and arms. The complete destruction of Chideock Castle was ordered and all the remaining building stone was later robbed. Thus some imagination is needed to picture the castle with its gatehouse. However, the moat which surrounded it, plus weathered ditches and humps in the ground remain, indicating fishponds and building platforms. *Chideock car park, DT6 6JQ, SY423927. Turn right and then first left up Ruins Lane. Continue for 100m along the footpath. The site is marked with a wooden cross.*

Chideock Castle.

Woodsford Castle William Whitfield was granted a licence to crenellate his manor house by Edward III in 1337. Its next owner, Sir Guy de Bryan, a close friend of Edward III, probably extended Woodsford's fortifications. Woodsford has been much altered over the centuries and three sides of it have disappeared, leaving it smaller and less martial than it was. The crenellations were lost when it was remodelled in the seventeenth century as a farmhouse with a very unmilitary thatched roof. The gatehouse and four towers have also been lost, though the north-east tower survives. However, other features also betray Woodsford's history as a fortified manor. Would-be intruders are denied easy entry: there are no doors on the east side and all the main rooms and larger windows are on the first floor. On the ground floor, the narrow openings were originally loops – useful for both archers and gunners. Moreover, the projecting stones on the north and east sides would have supported galleries for archers. *Woodsford Castle may be rented from the Landmark Trust, 01628 825920. SY758905, ½ mile west Woodsford village.*

Woodsford Castle.

Woodsford Castle, narrow window.

Athelhampton House is a fine example of a late medieval fortified manor. Sir William Martin obtained a licence from the newly crowned Henry VII in 1485 "to fortify his manor with walls of stone and lime and to build towers and crenellate them". Although Althelhampton's Tudor gatehouse was lost in 1862, the crenellations remain and are the oldest part of the house which, with its gardens, is open to the public. *Athelhampton House DT2 7LG, 01305 848363. On the Tolpuddle/Puddletown road at SY772945. athelhampton.co.uk*

Athelhampton House.

Wolfeton House is a handsome manor house with splendid plasterwork and panelling. It has a complex, layered history, beginning as an early sixteenth century courtyard house. Part of one range remains from this period. It was extended and embellished later in the sixteenth century, but there were demolitions and extensions in the nineteenth century. The Gatehouse (available for rent from the Landmark Trust) has two round towers and a date reset, 1534, whilst the South Tower has an embattled parapet and the topmost of its three stages dates from c1862. The crenellated north-east tower is nineteenth century. *Wolfeton House, Charminster, SY678921. Check opening times, 01305 263500.*

Wolfeton House.

From the outset, castles were nearly always residences as well as military redoubts. Moreover, the level of fortification between one castle and another and between one fortified manor and another, varied considerably. Like all medieval buildings they were essentially individual. Constructed with local materials to meet local needs, they were not made to any blueprint as most modern buildings are.

Defence remained a general need in Medieval England. Rebellion and civil war were repeated themes, thus castle building and repair continued, notably at Corfe Castle. A lesser known Dorset example is Marshwood Castle (visible from the public right of way at SW405977), where Edward III commissioned repairs in 1357. Earthworks, including a moat and rubble walls and part of an angle tower remain.

It was wise to defend key towns including Dorchester, where the Roman town wall was probably altered in medieval times and appears to have been at full strength until the Civil War. More pressing was the need to defend ports, especially during the Hundred Years War with France (1337-1453). Lyme and Poole were attacked in 1377; Melcombe Regis was burnt and destroyed. Portland was attacked in 1404. The worst assault was in 1405, when Poole was attacked and burnt after heavy fighting.

Poole was granted a licence for a wall in 1433 by Henry VI. Evidence for the town's defences is poor, apart from a ditch and a town gate, designed to protect Poole (almost a peninsula in medieval times) from landward attack. From the 1540s, Poole was better protected from seaborne raids by Brownsea Castle (page 31), which covered the harbour mouth, preventing enemy ships getting close.

Nationally, the political turmoil worsened during the 1450s and England was split between the Yorkist and Lancastrian factions. Warfare broke out in St Albans in 1453, only two years after the English were finally driven from France, ending the Hundred Years War and unleashing many battle hardened men on England. G.M. Trevelyan observed the Hundred Years War in France had "bred habits of violence at home". It also destabilised England and opened the way to more than thirty years of bloody civil war, later called the Wars of the Roses.

As in the later Civil War, Dorset was spared the major battles, which were fought around central England. They included Towton (1461), considered the bloodiest battle ever fought on English soil, Barnet (1471) and Tewkesbury (1471). The wars culminated at Bosworth in 1485. Archery and hand to hand combat with swords, knives, maces, flails and axes still decided the issue and accounted for most of the appalling casualties. Artillery and hand guns played a part, but they were not the decisive force in battle.

Tudor Fortifications, 1485 - 1603

After Richard III's defeat and death at Bosworth, Henry Tudor was crowned Henry VII. The Tudor period heralded a new era of warfare in which guns and powder began to augment and later supplant longbows and crossbows. Guns and powder also supplanted giant catapults and similar torsion weapons such as the trebuchet, which had been used since ancient times to both defend and attack fortifications, hurling rocks and incendiaries in both directions. On occasion, diseased corpses were also flung across the lines to demoralise the enemy and spread disease – sometimes the most deadly weapon of all.

Whilst torsion weapons could inflict considerable damage to castles and the people defending them, it was the growing capacity of gunpowder to destroy masonry from the sixteenth century onwards that rendered traditional castles far more vulnerable to attack. Artillery gradually improved in reliability, range and accuracy, whilst sappers developed the art of laying explosive charges in mines beneath castle walls. Perforce, the design of fortifications had to be radically re-thought. High walls had been a strong defence against enemies armed with ladders and siege towers. In the face of explosives, they were a liability. The solution was to build forts with low, thick walls and embrasures for guns, a design exemplified by Portland Castle. Despite the Tudor victory at Bosworth, rebellion – both secular and religious – remained a very real threat throughout the Tudor period. In the West Country, Perkin Warbeck's attempted coup in 1497 and the Prayer Book Rebellion of 1549 exposed the vulnerability of the new dynasty.

Foreign invasion was an even greater danger. France, England's traditional enemy, was much strengthened as a naval power through her union with Brittany in 1491. Spain, with her extensive empire and wealth, was a major threat on the world stage, especially once allied with France in 1538. Alarmed, Henry VIII (1509-47), commanded a string of twenty "device" forts built along England's south and east coasts in 1539. As a castle building king, Henry stands second only to William the Conqueror.

Henry's break with the Catholic Church also spurred him on. His fear of a religiously inspired Reconquista, similar to the Catholic Crusade against the Moors in Spain, was well founded. By divorcing his first wife, Catherine of Aragon, he had profoundly insulted all Catholic nations, especially Spain as Catherine was Charles V's aunt. Henry compounded his offences in the eyes of his enemies by dissolving monasteries and other religious houses. He used some of the enormous funds raised for his emergency fort building programme.

Apart from their guns and gun platforms, what made all these Tudor coastal forts different from medieval castles was that they were designed for national defence, not to subdue a conquered people as in the first phase of Norman castle building. Neither were they designed to defend powerful aristocrats and express their power within the county, nor to protect Royal power against a dangerous aristocracy.

> **Sandsfoot Castle** was partly built with stone from the recently suppressed Bindon Abbey (near Wool) and completed in 1542. It occupies a strong position on a cliff overlooking Weymouth Bay and the Portland Roads, facing Portland Castle across this strategically vital harbour – an obvious landing point for an invasion force. Two castles were needed due to the limited range of guns at the time. They proved their worth in deterring attack during the Spanish Armada crisis of 1588, when English ships drove off Spanish warships in the Battle of Portland just east of the Isle. They served the same role in the seventeenth century Anglo-Dutch Wars.
>
> Portland and Sandsfoot's designs differed: Sandsfoot was a square blockhouse with a facetted gun emplacement on the seaward side, while Portland's two storey gun tower has a curved front gun emplacement. Sandsfoot's landward defences were added about the time of the Spanish Armada to protect it from an enemy landing further along the coast and attack from the rear. Still partly extant, these defences consisted of an open earthen barbican with an external ditch to protect the main entrance. The

Sandsfoot Castle.

earthworks would have been strengthened with a wooden palisade to protect infantry and possibly stone filled gabions to protect artillery. Domestic quarters for Sandsfoot's garrison included the still extant fireplaces. There was also a kitchen, hall, sleeping quarters and garderobes. Munitions and stores were kept in the basement.

Sandsfoot was held for Parliament at the start of the Civil War, reflecting Weymouth's Parliamentarian sympathies. However, when the Earl of Carnarvon entered Dorset with his Royalist army in 1643, Weymouth surrendered and Sandsfoot was held by the Royalists until the Earl of Essex retook Dorset for Parliament in 1644.

After 124 years of service, Sandsfoot was removed from the military register in 1665 and used as a store. In 1701 it was stripped of some of its stone to build Weymouth's town bridge. Stone robbing and cliff falls caused further damage, but Sandsfoot is now protected and open to the public. *Signed from A354. Old Castle Road, Weymouth, DT4 8QG, SY675775. Open during daylight.*

Portland Castle.

Portland Castle is Sandsfoot's sister castle and built at the same time. Both are better described as gun forts and reflected the most advanced military design of the time. Portland's low walls offer only a shallow target but, like the walls at Sandsfoot, they are strongly built and 12ft (nearly 4m) thick to resist blast. Originally, it had two gun floors, each with five guns. In time of war, each gun was served by a team of four or five men and the castle's full complement of soldiers was raised to one hundred, though in times of peace fifteen men were enough to garrison it.

The castle only saw action during the Civil War. Initially held by Royalists, it was captured in 1643 by Parliamentarians. However, the Royalists recaptured it with a clever ruse after only three days. A group of sixty Royalists disguised as Parliamentarians pretended to be pursued by their comrades. Deceived, the Roundhead garrison admitted them and were overpowered. In 1646, after a four month siege which included artillery exchanges, lack of supplies forced the castle's Royalist garrison to surrender. They were allowed to leave with full military honours.

Portland Castle was last armed as a coastal gun fort during the Napoleonic Wars, though it was used in combatting smuggling and privateering in the nineteenth century. During the First World War it was used as an arms store and in the Second World War as accommodation for soldiers and WRENS. *English Heritage, 01305 820539, DT5 1AZ. Signed from A354, SY686745. www.english-heritage.org.uk*

Brownsea Castle.

Brownsea Castle began as a blockhouse and is contemporary with Sandsfoot and Portland Castles, though not recorded until 1547. It had walls 13m (42ft)square and almost 3m (10ft) thick. Defended on the three landward sides by a moat, it had a hexagonal gun platform on the seaward side. The cost of building and manning the castle (again, better described as a gun fort) was borne by Poole, although Queen Elizabeth I funded new guns and powder. It was held for Parliament during the Civil War, but saw no action. After 1710, a series of wealthy owners altered Brownsea Castle, which lost several turrets and other features after a fire in 1896, though part of the original castle survives in the basement. Now closed to the public, it can be viewed from the sea by taking the Brownsea Island ferry. The island is open through the National Trust. *Brownsea Island Boats 01929 462383 from Poole Quay (BH15 1HJ) or Sandbanks (BH13 7QN). National Trust 01202 707744 . www.nationaltrust.org.uk/brownsea-island*

The Civil Wars, 1642 - 1651

Dorset's Tudor gun forts were garrisoned during the Civil Wars and Portland Castle (page 30) endured a four month siege on the medieval pattern. These forts were designed in the age of artillery, but Corfe, Sherborne, Christchurch and Chideock Castles, which were all attacked during the Civil War, pre-dated artillery.

Nonetheless, Dorset's ancient fortifications acquitted themselves well. Christchurch Castle proved too strong for the troop of 1,000 Royalists who attacked the town in January 1645 and besieged the castle with artillery for three days. Corfe withstood two long sieges with artillery and only succumbed through treachery (page 20). Artillery, however, was decisive in taking Sherborne Old Castle after sixteen days siege (page 16) and Chideock Castle was taken and retaken several times.

Victorian Fortifications

Well sheltered by Chesil Beach and the Portland peninsula, Portland Harbour is a superb natural haven of prime strategic value. Large enough to accommodate the Grand Fleet, it sheltered up to 200 head of sail in Victorian times and remained a key anchorage for the Royal Navy until the late twentieth century. As in Henry VIII's era, Portland Harbour was seen as a possible point for foreign invasion. Thus it was doubly important to protect Portland Harbour from both landward and seaward attack in the same way as other vital naval bases, including Plymouth and Portsmouth.

The last major phase of fortifying Dorset began in 1849 when Prince Albert laid the foundation stone of Portland Breakwater to protect its only exposed side, the east. Portland and Weymouth's system of breakwaters and forts developed greatly over the following 75 years, whilst the perceived threats to Britain grew and military science advanced. It was a massive task, involving teams of engineers and craftsmen, plus the construction of miles of railways and inclined planes to transport Portland Stone to the various building sites. Convicts from Portland Prison provided much of the hard labour, while tourists flocked to see this wonder of British engineering.

The Inner and Outer Breakwater arms were completed in 1872. Once the harbour's vulnerability to torpedoes was realised, the Middle and Bincleaves arms were added. Work was completed in 1906, making Portland the largest artificial harbour in the world. Finally, the vulnerable South Ship Channel was blocked by scuttling the obsolete HMS Hood across its mouth on November 4, 1914, three months after the outbreak of war.

Outer or Chequer Breakwater Fort, Portland.

  Meanwhile, forts were built to ring the harbour. Upton Fort near Osmington Mills and Nothe Fort at Weymouth covered the northern side. On the Isle of Portland, Verne Citadel with its High Angle Battery was the key defence, supported by East Wears and West Wears Forts. The Inner Breakwater Forts guarded the harbour's entrance.

  We anticipate: work had barely begun on Verne Citadel when the French navy launched the first ocean going ironclad warship, *Gloire* in 1859, causing consternation in Britain, which still viewed France as the national enemy and regarded Emperor Napoleon III with suspicion. Moreover, Britain prided itself on being the world's leading naval power since the victory of Trafalgar in 1805 and *Gloire* was an insult to nationalist sentiment as well as a tangible threat. Armed with explosive shells and the latest rifled guns – far more accurate than smooth bore artillery – and proof against the most powerful British guns of the time, *Gloire* rendered traditional unarmoured wooden ships of the line obsolete.

  The Royal Navy responded in 1860 by launching HMS *Warrior*, the world's first iron-hulled ironclad warship. Meanwhile, Lord Palmerston, the British Prime Minister, set up a Royal Commission on the Defence of the United Kingdom. Despite a strenuous debate in Parliament about whether the expense of a major fort building programme was justified, the most costly system of fixed defences built in Britain during peacetime went ahead. It had parallels with Henry VIII's "device" fort programme, but was even more extensive. The "Palmerston Forts" project included places as far apart as Belfast, Alderney, the Clyde and Milford Haven.

No French attack materialised and Germany, which began a naval shipbuilding race with Britain from 1898, emerged as the new enemy. During the First and Second World Wars Portland's forts proved their worth as coastal defences and, in some cases, anti-aircraft sites. Supplemented with searchlight batteries, anti-tank defences and pillboxes, Portland and Weymouth played important roles in defending the coast from invasion in 1940 and in the D Day preparations, 1943/44.

Breakwater Forts The larger Outer Breakwater Fort is 116ft (35m) in diameter and built of granite with a box girder construction, armoured walls and a bomb proof iron roof. Operational from 1882, its four 12.5 inch muzzle loading guns were replaced with 6 inch breech loaders, quick firing guns and a Maxim machine gun in 1907. During the Second World War, its anti-aircraft guns often fired on German aircraft attacking ships in the harbour. Throughout the war, the fort was gallantly supplied by MV *My Girl*, which still sails from Weymouth Harbour and is one of several vessels giving visitors a chance to see the Breakwater Forts close up and gain an excellent view of Nothe Fort.

Part of the Breakwater Fort, Portland.

Nothe Fort Nothe headland guards the entrance to Weymouth Harbour. Guns were sited on Nothe from the mid-sixteenth century and a small fort was added during the Civil War. In 1645, when Weymouth was occupied by Royalist forces for a time, cannons on Nothe fired into Melcombe, causing "great damage to houses and buildings in the town". The much larger Palmerston fort we see today was begun in 1860. Built of large mortared blocks of Portland Stone, granite and brick and supported by heavy earth banks to absorb shock, it was completed in 1872. At casemate level, the walls are 12-13ft (4m) thick, but at the lower magazine levels the thickness is 50ft (15m).

Designed in a semi-circle reminiscent of medieval castle fer de cheval (horseshoe) towers, it had a wide field of fire. On the landward side there are several other features borrowed from medieval castles. Until 1938, the fort was guarded by a drawbridge, manually operated by a winch. It was also protected by a glacis (slope) and a dry ditch (moat), numerous loop holes for muskets and a caponier to provide enfilading fire along the ditch. The entrance was further defended by the Barbican, complete with machicolations, an iron gate and musket slots.

Nothe Fort was initially armed with two 64 lb, four 9 inch and six 10 inch muzzle loading, rifled guns. Artillery science advanced rapidly. Massive 12.5 inch guns were introduced in the 1890s, followed by three 6 inch breech loading guns and two quick firing guns in 1912. These had more firepower than all the previous muzzle loaders combined. None of these guns saw action. However, a 40mm Bofors gun was fired in anger

World War Two guns at Nothe Fort.

during World War Two, as were four 3.7 inch anti-aircraft guns stationed in what is now the car park. Backed by field lights, they attacked German bombers en route to Bristol, as well as defending Weymouth and Portland, especially important during D Day operations. The fort also served as an ammunition store during the war.

Allow time for the fort's many interesting displays, most relating to coastal defence and local military history. It also has a programme of historical re-enactments and gun firings. *Nothe Fort, Barrack Road, Weymouth, DT4 8UF, 01305 766626. www.nothefort.org.uk*

Nothe Fort from the sea.

Verne Citadel and the High Angle Batteries Verne Citadel was built between 1857 and 1881, with the East Wears Battery providing its outworks and West Wears (Blacknor) Fort providing additional protection from 1902. Sited on Portland's highest point, 500ft (152m) above sea level, Verne Citadel commands wide views over Weymouth Bay and Portland Harbour. Moreover, it is naturally inaccessible from the north and east.

Its potential was recognised by the Romans, who sited a station and fort there. Covering 56 acres (23ha), Verne Citadel was built as a siege fortress to accommodate 500 troops, later increased to 1,000. By 1903, it had lost its defensive role and was used as an infantry barracks. Its guns were removed in 1906 and it became the HQ of Coast Artillery during the World Wars. After 1937, Verne Citadel was used as an infantry training centre. Radar was installed and the main magazine became a hospital.

From 1949 to 2013, Verne served as a prison and at the time of writing is an immigration removal centre.

The best preserved of its type in Britain, Verne's High Angle Battery was built around 1892 to house six, 9 inch rifled muzzle loading guns. These fired heavy shells at high angles over the cliffs and onto the decks of enemy ships, which were much more vulnerable than the heavily armoured sides. The guns were mounted on turntables, allowing them to rotate through 360 degrees. Ammunition was stored in underground magazines for safety and protection. The shells were delivered to the guns via a system of rails, ramps and a bridge, allowing them to arrive at muzzle height for direct loading. As well as the gun emplacements and magazines, the earth mound covering the laboratory and a large bombproof shelter for troops is extant. *Verne High Angle Battery, signed from A354 south of Chiswell, SY695734.*

The Verne High-Angle Battery.

Upton Fort Built between 1901 and 1903, Upton Fort near Osmington Mills completed the defensive ring around Portland Harbour and Weymouth. It was armed with two 6 inch breech loading guns. Rearmed to operate as an emergency battery in 1940-41, it was equipped with two Coastal Artillery Searchlights, plus a 40mm Bofors gun and ground defences, including machine guns. Many buildings survive on the 5½ acre (2.3ha) site, but this is on private land and partly covered by scrub. *Upton Fort, SY740815. Elements may be viewed from the Coast Path.*

Part of Upton Fort from the coastpath.

Dorchester Keep Military Museum The Keep is a Victorian Gothic version of a medieval gatehouse. Built in Portland Stone and replete with towers, crenellations and arrow slits, it was completed in 1879. Originally the gatehouse for the Depot Barracks of the Dorsetshire Regiment and the County Armoury, its military service ended in 1958, but it found a new life as the museum of the Devon and Dorset Regiments and has much to offer anyone interested in military history. *Barrack Road, Dorchester DT1 1RN, 01305 264066. www.keepmilitarymuseum.org*

Dorchester Keep.

Second World War Fortifications

Upton Fort, Nothe Fort and Portland's Breakwater Forts were armed and saw action during the Second World War, Dorchester's Keep was used for military recruitment and training; Verne Citadel too was used for training, whilst Portland Castle accommodated service personnel. Tyneham village and the Lulworth Ranges were requisitioned for D Day training in 1943 and are still under MOD control with limited public access.

Many smaller fortifications were built to deter and combat invasion and protect personnel training for D Day. Some survive, mainly on the coast, but also inland, sometimes in surprising places such as the pillbox in Woodsford Castle's garden. A 2km (1.3 mile) walk around Studland includes Dragon's Teeth anti-tank defences at Middle Beach (SZ036830); Fort Henry observation bunker (SZ037828 - used by Churchill, Eisenhower and King George VI to watch D Day training); the Bankes Arms (a control base) and the concrete pillbox on South Beach (SZ038828). Download a route description www.nationaltrust.org.uk/studlandbeach/trails/studland-beach-second-world-war-walk.

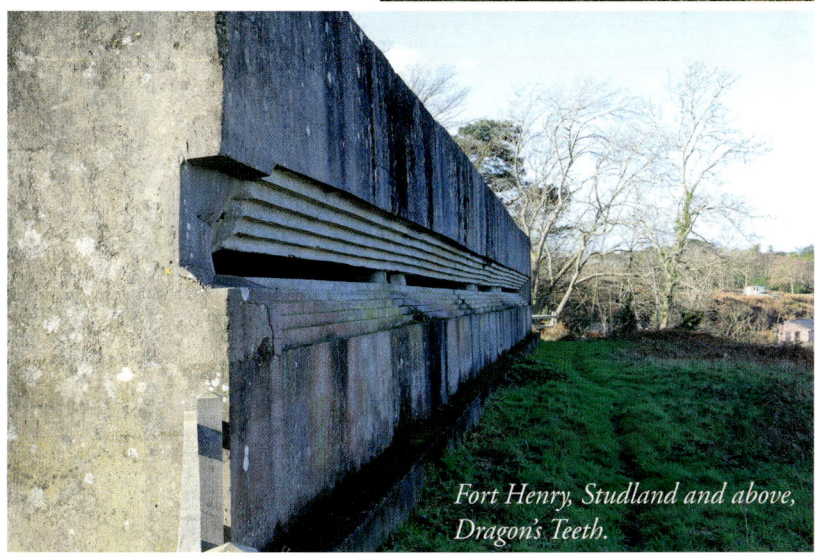

Fort Henry, Studland and above, Dragon's Teeth.

Castles as Luxury Homes

Owning a castle has always been associated with power and prestige. Thus it is hardly surprising that some high status houses are called "castles" even though they were not designed for defence. Often they are embellished with characteristic castle features such as towers and crenellations,

Brownsea Castle (page 31) is a prime example of these embellishments, though admittedly it began as a Tudor gun fort and incorporates elements of that fort in its present unmilitary incarnation. Similarly, the magnificent symmetrical towers of seventeenth century Lulworth Castle were designed to impress. Highcliffe Castle is built in the nineteenth century Gothic Revival style, whilst Durlston Castle's towers with their arrow slits and observation posts are Victorian Gothic and entirely decorative.

Lulworth Castle.

Lulworth Castle The castle we see today is not the Lulworth Castle taken by Robert of Gloucester in 1142 during the Anarchy of King Stephen's troubled reign. Nothing is known of the design of that castle and it may not have been on the site of the present castle, which was built by Viscount Bindon in 1608. A perfect cube 80ft square, it was designed primarily as a hunting lodge, and one magnificent enough to entertain King James I when he hunted in the Purbecks. Humphrey Weld bought it in 1641, but shortly left to join King Charles in Oxford. Parliamentarians seized Lulworth Castle and stripped it of lead to make musket balls for the siege of Corfe Castle. Weld restored Lulworth Castle as the family seat, but it was gutted by fire in 1929. Happily, the exterior has been carefully restored.

Visitors can enjoy magnificent views from the battlements and study the castle's history through tableaux and film. *Lulworth Castle, East Lulworth BH20 5QS, SY856822, 0845 450 1054. www.lulworth.com.*

Durlston Castle (and right).

Highcliffe Castle.

Highcliffe Castle
Constructed in the 1830s with materials salvaged from medieval French buildings, Highcliffe Castle gives the impression of being much older than it really is. An outstanding example of Romantic Picturesque architecture, it has been beautifully restored after fire damage and is a venue for art exhibitions and weddings. Several rooms are open to the public, as are its gardens, which reach to the sea. *Highcliffe Castle, Rothesay Drive, Highcliffe, Christchurch, BH23 4LE, SZ203932, 01425 278807. www.highcliffecastle.co.uk*

Durlston Castle
Durlston Castle was built in 1887 as a restaurant for visitors to George Burt's Durlston Estate, now Durlston Country Park. There are fine views of the coast from the rooftop; a shop, an art gallery and a visitor centre with wildlife exhibits and tableaux. *Durlston Castle, Swanage, BH19 2JL, SZ033774, 01929 424443. www.durlston.co.uk*

Key to Locations

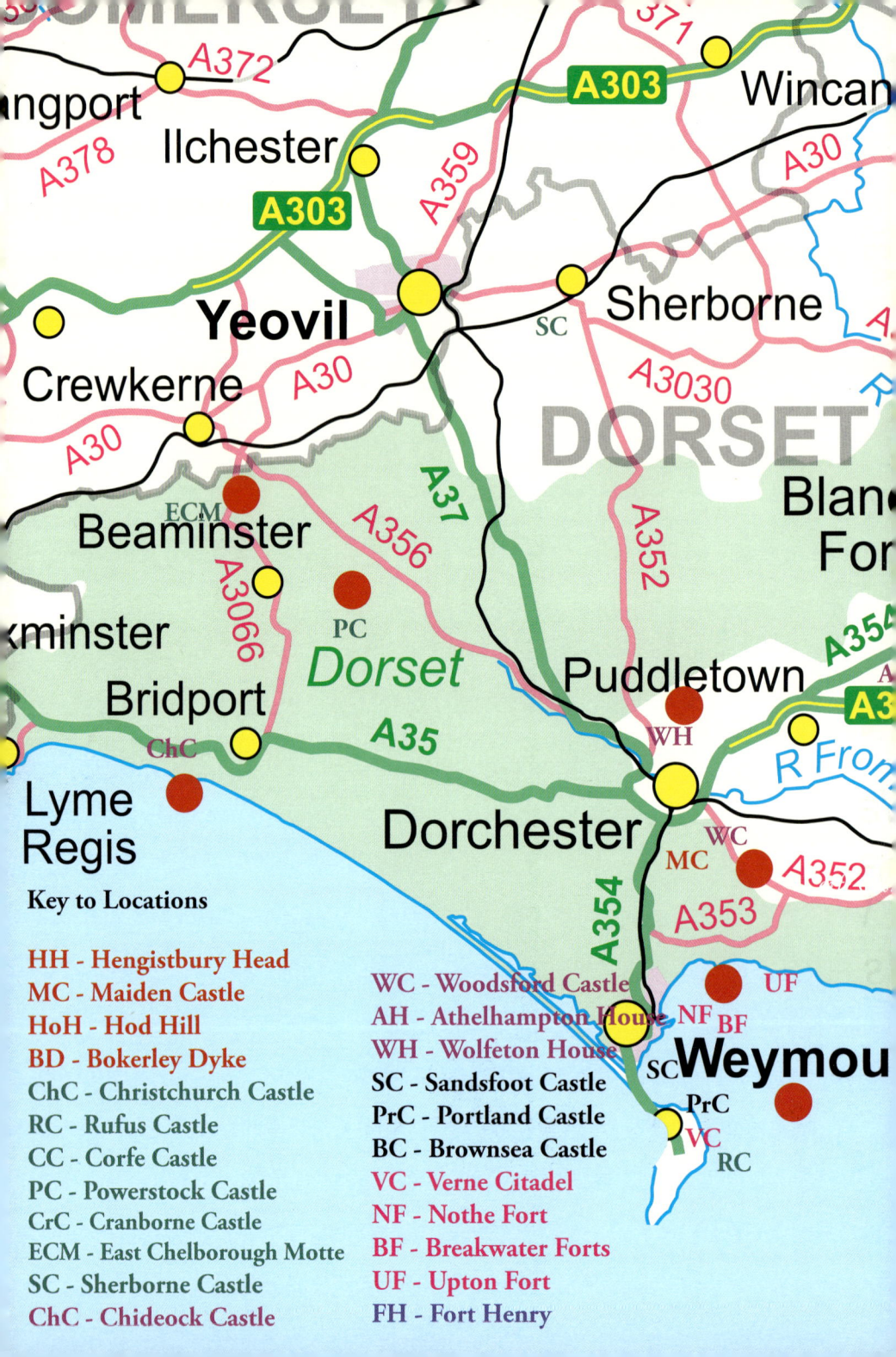

HH - Hengistbury Head
MC - Maiden Castle
HoH - Hod Hill
BD - Bokerley Dyke
ChC - Christchurch Castle
RC - Rufus Castle
CC - Corfe Castle
PC - Powerstock Castle
CrC - Cranborne Castle
ECM - East Chelborough Motte
SC - Sherborne Castle
ChC - Chideock Castle

WC - Woodsford Castle
AH - Athelhampton House
WH - Wolfeton House
SC - Sandsfoot Castle
PrC - Portland Castle
BC - Brownsea Castle
VC - Verne Citadel
NF - Nothe Fort
BF - Breakwater Forts
UF - Upton Fort
FH - Fort Henry

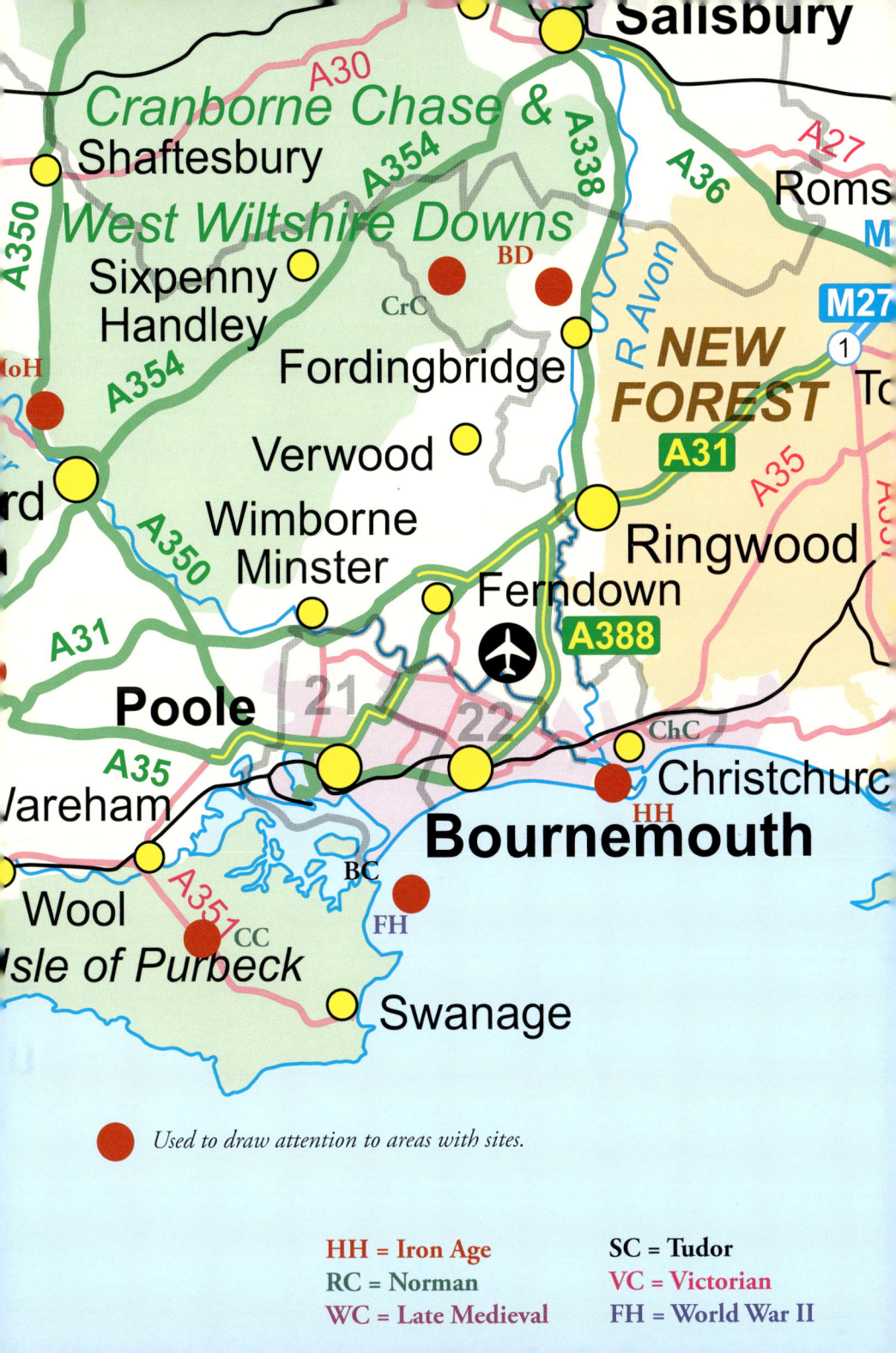

HH = Iron Age
RC = Norman
WC = Late Medieval
SC = Tudor
VC = Victorian
FH = World War II

Used to draw attention to areas with sites.

Select Bibliography

Hesketh, Robert, *Tales of the Dorset Coast*, Inspiring Places Publishing, Alderholt, 2015.

Hesketh, Robert, *A Guide to the Beaches and Coves of Dorset*, Inspiring Places Publishing, Alderholt, 2012.

Pomeroy, Colin, *Discover Dorset Castles and Forts*, Dovecote Press, Wimborne, 1998.

Salter, Mike, *The Castles of Wessex*, Folly Publications, Malvern, 2002.

Westwood, Robert, *Ancient Dorset*, Inspiring Places Publishing, Alderholt, 2015.

Westwood, Robert, *Tales of Historic Dorset,* Inspiring Places Publishing, Alderholt, 2015.

Wilton, Phil, *Castles of Dorset*, Phil Wilton Publishing, Wimborne, 1995.

Other Dorset titles by Inspiring Places:

Ancient Dorset
Tales of Historic Dorset
Tales of the Dorset Coast
Legends and Folklore of Dorset
The Story of Tyneham
A Guide to the Beaches and Coves of Dorset
The Railway Heritage of Dorset and Somerset
Secret Dorset
Fossils and Rocks of the Jurassic Coast
Jurassic Coast Fossils
Great Houses and Gardens of Dorset
The Life and Works of Thomas Hardy
Walking West Dorset
Purbeck Walks
A brief guide to Purbeck
A brief guide to Sherborne, Shaftesbury and Blandford
A brief guide to Dorchester, Weymouth and Portland

www.inspiringplaces.co.uk